21st Century
Basic Skills
Library

LET'S SORT BY COLOR

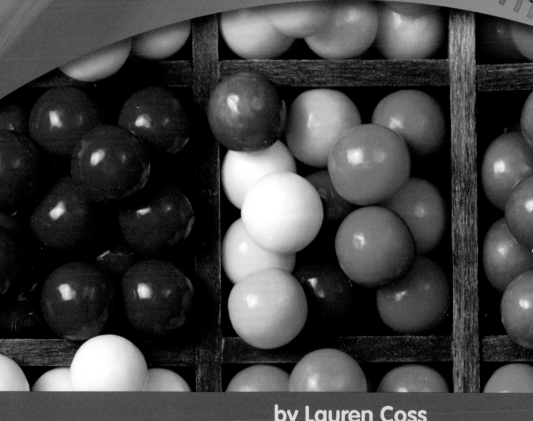

by Lauren Coss

Cherry Lake Publishing • Ann Arbor, Michigan

2

Published in the United States of America
by Cherry Lake Publishing
Ann Arbor, Michigan
www.cherrylakepublishing.com

Consultant: Marla Conn, ReadAbility, Inc.
Editorial direction and book production: Red Line Editorial
Book design and illustration: Design Lab

Photo Credits: Jenn Huls/Shutterstock Images, cover, 1; Robert Kneschke/
Shutterstock Images, 4; Sirikorn Thamniyom/Shutterstock Images, 6 (left), 6 (right);
Kuzma/Shutterstock Images, 8; Sonya Etchison/Shutterstock Images, 10; Africa
Studio/Shutterstock Images, 12 (top), 12 (bottom); Monkey Business Images/
Shutterstock Images, 14; sjhuls/iStock/Thinkstock, 16; Goodshoot/Thinkstock, 18;
somchaij/Shutterstock Images, 20

Library of Congress Cataloging-in-Publication Data
Coss, Lauren, author.
  Let's sort by color / by Lauren Coss ; consultant: Marla Conn, ReadAbility, Inc.
      pages cm. -- (Sorting)
  Audience: Age 6.
  Audience: Grades K to 3.
  Includes index.
  ISBN 978-1-63137-634-4 (hardcover) -- ISBN 978-1-63137-679-5 (pbk.) -- ISBN 978-
1-63137-724-2 (pdf ebook) -- ISBN 978-1-63137-769-3 (hosted ebook)
  1. Colors--Juvenile literature. 2. Set theory--Juvenile literature. I. Title. II. Title: Let us
sort by color.

  QC495.5.C674 2014
  535.6--dc23
                                                    2014004572

Cherry Lake Publishing would like to acknowledge the work of The Partnership for
21st Century Skills. Please visit *www.p21.org* for more information.

Printed in the United States of America
Corporate Graphics Inc.
July 2014

TABLE OF CONTENTS

5   **What Is Sorting?**

11   **The Market**

15   **Button Bunches**

19   **Rainbow Crayons**

22   Find Out More

22   Glossary

23   Home and School Connection

24   Index

24   About the Author

What Is Sorting?

Sorting means putting **alike** things together.

Let's try sorting by color.

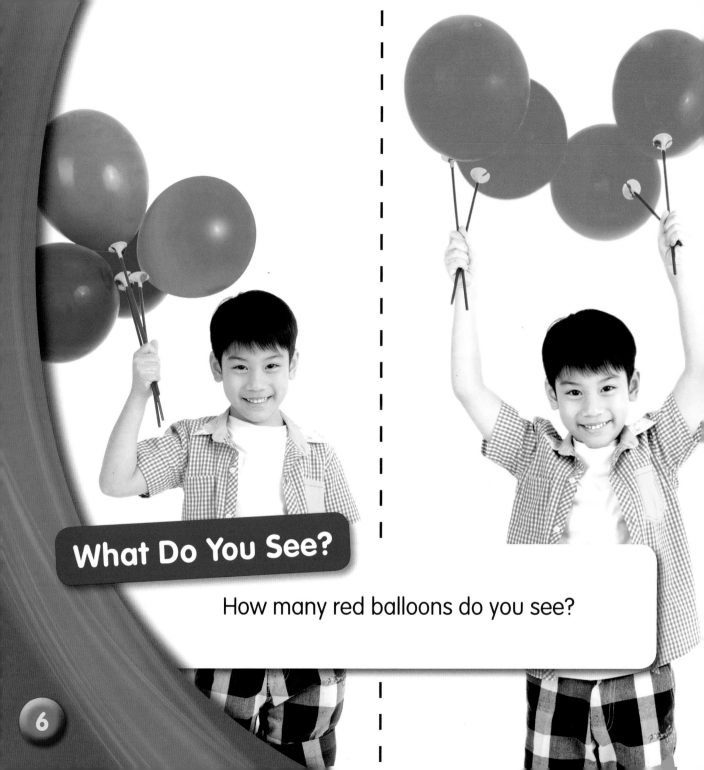

What Do You See?

How many red balloons do you see?

Some of Jake's balloons are blue.

He sorts them into a blue group.

Red balloons go into a red group.

One balloon does not belong in this group.

Which balloon is **different**?

What Do You See?

What color is the tomato Jen is holding?

The Market

The market has healthy foods.

Some foods are red. Others are green.

Help Jen sort these yummy foods by color.

Now the foods are sorted by color.

All the foods in each group are the same color.

Button Bunches

Lily has many buttons.

Let's sort her buttons by color.

15

What Do You See?

How many colors of buttons do you see?

The yellow buttons are different **shades**.

But they are all yellow.

Lily sorts them into the yellow group.

Rainbow Crayons

A **rainbow** has colors in a certain order.

It goes red, orange, yellow, green, blue, **indigo**, **violet**.

Let's sort the crayons to match the rainbow.

Look around!

What can you sort by color?

Find Out More

BOOK

Peppas, Lynn. *Sorting*. New York: Crabtree Publishing, 2009.

WEB SITE

Freezer Burn Snack Sort
www.pbskids.org/lunchlab/?level=2#/games/escape-from-greasy-world
Practice your sorting skills with this fun game.

Glossary

alike (uh-LIKE) the same

different (DIF-ur-uhnt) not the same

indigo (IN-di-goh) a dark purplish-blue color

rainbow (RAYN-boh) an arc of colors caused by bending sunlight

shades (SHAYDZ) the darkness of colors

violet (VYE-uh-lit) a light blue-purple color

Home and School Connection

Use this list of words from the book to help your child become a better reader. Word games and writing activities can help beginning readers reinforce literacy skills.

alike	different	orange	things
balloons	foods	order	together
blue	green	rainbow	tomato
bunches	group	red	violet
button	healthy	same	yellow
certain	indigo	shades	yummy
color	market	sort	
crayons	match		

What Do You See?

What Do You See? is a feature paired with select photos in this book. It encourages young readers to interact with visual images in order to build the ability to integrate content in various media formats.

You can help your child further evaluate photos in this book with additional activities. Look at the images in the book without the What Do You See? feature. Ask your child to describe one detail in each image, such as a color, activity, or setting.

Index

alike, 5

balloons, 6, 7, 9
blue, 7, 19
buttons, 15, 16, 17

crayons, 21

different, 9, 17

foods, 11, 13

green, 11, 19
groups, 7, 9, 13, 17

indigo, 19

market, 11

orange, 19

rainbows, 19, 21
red, 6, 7, 11, 19

shades, 17

violet, 19

yellow, 17, 19

About the Author

Lauren Coss is an editor and author who lives in Minneapolis, Minnesota. Her favorite colors are blue and green.